William Robson Arrowsmith

Shakespeare's Editors and Commentators

William Robson Arrowsmith

Shakespeare's Editors and Commentators

ISBN/EAN: 9783337063412

Printed in Europe, USA, Canada, Australia, Japan

Cover: Foto ©Thomas Meinert / pixelio.de

More available books at **www.hansebooks.com**

SHAKESPEARE'S

EDITORS AND COMMENTATORS.

BY THE

REV. W. R. ARROWSMITH,

INCUMBENT OF OLD ST. PANCRAS.

LONDON:

J. RUSSELL SMITH, 36, SOHO SQUARE.

1865.

CHAPTER I.

In a letter to Nicholas Okes the printer, inserted at the end of Heywood's "Apology for Actors," a treatise published in 1612, speaking of William Jaggard the writer observes, "The infinite faults escaped in my booke of Britaines Troy by the negligence of the printer, as the misquotations, mistaking of syllables, misplacing half lines, coining of strange and never heard of words, these being without number, when I would have taken a particular account of the *Errata*, the printer answered me, hee would not publish his owne disworkmanship, but rather let his owne fault lye upon the necke of the author."

Now, whatever reason Heywood had to feel himself aggrieved, a comparison of his Troja Britannica,*

* Mr. Dyce appears not to be acquainted with this poem of Heywood's, or he would hardly have ventured the bold assertion : —"I have therefore not the slightest doubt that wherever 'statue' occurs, while the metre requires three syllables, it is an error for 'statua.' Our old poets no more thought of using 'statue' as a trisyllable than 'stature,' a third form of the word which is not unfrequently found." Note 102. P. 217 of Vol. 5. Ed. 1864. For, notwithstanding Heywood's fretful outburst at his printer's carelessness and selfish perversity, "statue" never occurs in the Troja Britannica as a trisyllable, but it has the diæresis, *e.g.* :—

4

printed by William, with the first Folio Shakspeare,
printed by Isaac Jaggard, will show that the like
complaint might far more truly have been preferred

> Of marble statuës many thousand more. Cant. 5. St. 111.
> Two hundred of his traine his eye hath scene
> All statuës. Cant. 6. St. 42.
> Placing his statuë that his prayse did sing,
> In Romes hye Capitoll. Cant. 8. St. 10.
> On which Apolloes statuë dwels for aye. Cant. 10. St. 46.

Besides, in Note (50) to Love's Labour's Lost. P. 243-4 of
Vol. 2, after reporting that, " Whitely (in the old eds. 'whitly'*),
has been considered by some critics as a questionable reading,
Rosaline being, as we learn from several places of the play, dark-
complexioned,"—critics, by superlative euphemism thus named, so
devoid of all judgment as to deem " whitely" akin to fair, although,
if common observation may be our guide, whiteness, whether by
contrast or not, is a peculiar attribute of dark features,—Mr. Dyce
proceeds to remark that, " on the other hand Walker (Crit. Exam.
&c. Vol. 2, p. 349), cites the line with the reading 'whitely:'"
and quotes from North's Plutarch, " lean and whitely-faced
fellow:" whence two things may be concluded, one, that the epithet
"whitely" is not rare, since it was picked up by Walker in a
note of Malone's, on a passage in Act 2. Scene 9, of the Merchant of Venice, without any suspicion by that critic that it would
ever be wanted to support the authentic reading in Love's
Labour's Lost ; another, and that which has provoked the present
mooting of a point to be discussed hereafter, that Mr. Dyce is
evidently not aware that this adjective " whitely" occurs in Cant.
5. St. 74, of the Troja Britannica :—

> " That hath a whitely face, and a long nose,
>   And for them both I wonderous well esteeme her."

Which lines do not merely furnish an instance of the epithet
"whitely," but, in such company as parallels Shakespeare's

---

* Misprinted in the Camb. Ed. "whitley."

by Heminge and Condell against the latter, even
after every allowance is made for the greater
liability to mistake in the persons, their exits and
entrances, the multifarious dialogue, the broken sentences, and varied phraseology of a play. It would
therefore be manifest injustice to fasten upon the
editors of the Folio 1623 blunders for which its
printer Jaggard is clearly accountable, or in any
measure to make those a ground for impugning the
good faith of its somewhat partial representation, that
" where (before) you were abused with diuerse stolne,
and surreptitious copies, maimed, and deformed by
the frauds and stealthes of iniurious impostors, that
expos'd them: euen those, are now offer'd to your
view cur'd and perfect of their limbes; and all the
rest, absolute in their numbers, as he conceiued thē.

coupling of it with " a wanton." If the pertinency of this argu-
ment be lost upon " some critics," it only adds further proof,
where none is needed, that they have no pretensions to that
name, nor the faintest calling to interfere with Shakespeare's
text: for their enlightenment, however, it may be stated that
though "whitely" and "fair" be not near allied, "wanton-
ness" and " a long nose" are, at least in our early dramatic writers,
from whom principally old readings must be made good. That
Mr. Collier should turn "whitely" into "witty" discloses more
puerility of artifice than defect of knowledge; while its trans-
formation into "wightly" by the Cambridge editors should be a
warning to them and their compeers not to embark in novelties,
nor quit their proper province, but stick to the drudgery of
collating and compiling, for which they may not be meanly qualified, and forbear to intrude upon even the outskirts of the domains
of philology, wherein they have neither part nor lot.

—And what he thought, he vttered with that easinesse,
that wee have scarce receiued from him a blot in his
papers"—yet how many annotators, how many editors
of Shakespeare, down to the present time, visit the
sins of Jaggard upon Heminge and Condell; do by
them what Heywood deprecated with respect to
himself, "let the faults of the printer lie upon their
necks." And because "the dram of base doth all
the noble substance often draw to his own scandal,"
hence the slur derived from the printing-house upon
their credit as editors has left no parts of their work
free from question; sound and unsound alike have
in turn been doubted, and tampered with: the up-
shot is, that in many places Shakespeare's genuine
language has been discarded, and the text alloyed
with adulterate mixtures; exclusive of that long
array of unvitiated readings whereof the meaning has
been balked. The customary speech, and syntax of
the 16th century are sometimes supplanted, another
while hybridised, every where measured by a diction
and syntax prevalent in the 17th, 18th and 19th; a
mishap to some extent unavoidable, because the
dialect of yesterday, to-day, and to-morrow, under-
goes a change so gradual that it is not noted; varia-
tion is lost in resemblance; and to Englishmen reading English an obsolete style is still unconsciously
identified with each successive ever-widening diver-
gence from it: but such has been the illiterate pedan-
try of officious notemongers that sentences of a construction not less current now than 260 years ago are

evermore cavilled at, and either misexpounded, or if
the true sense be hit, the words are wrenched, and
sprained, and untruly sorted. An ill-printed book,
but above all, minds unseasoned with Elizabethan
literature have wrought the biggest half of this mis-
chief; the only remedy for it is, what many students,
many interpreters, and not a few editors of Shakespeare sadly lack—reading, extensive reading, to
quell meddlesomeness, and beget self-distrust. By
dint of that Englishmen will begin to comprehend,
how huge is the debt of gratitude owed by their
countrymen to Heminge and Condell.

A little taste at the outset will be enough to evince
that Shakespeare, to be understood, must be read in
the light, and by one habituated to the light of his
times: thus, to 'occupy' and to 'do,' verbs that
in the reign of Elizabeth and her successor were
suggestive of "most maculate thoughts," have long
lost the ambiguous import, which ribald pleasantry
for a season lent them, and now, as of yore,—as
when Shakespeare was a boy,—may be uttered in
ears never so captious, without risk of perversion;
and although "soon" in the west of England to this
day, as is said,* still signifies "evening," yet elsewhere, or to persons unversed in the nomenclature
of the Tudor-Stuart æra, such a signification is un-
known, and would be sought to as little purpose in
the Minsheus† of a prior, or a later date, as in the

---

* Halliwell's Dictionary of Archaic and Provincial Words.

† Minsheu's Ductor in linguas.

grammar of a Bullokar or a Murray would the fact, attested by a contemporary of Shakespeare, a Head-Master of St. Paul's School,—that the use of " soon" as an adverb, in the familiar sense of "betimes," " by and by," or " quickly," had, when he wrote, been eclipsed with most men by an acceptation restricted to " nightfall :" the statement of this witness is worth quoting in his own words. In the comparison of adverbs, at page 28 of his Logonomia Anglica, ed. 1619, Gil writes — " Quickly cito, sooner citior aut citius, soonest citissimus aut citissime, nam ' soon' hodie apud plurimos significat ad primam vesperam, olim cito."

Bating errors of the Press, most of which an average English scholar might, as he reads, amend for himself; and forgiving Jaggard his execution of a task from MS., which the reprint of 1807 failed to match from letter-press, it is a great treat to ramble over the Folio, photolithographed by Day, without let or rub of notes, wherewith bile, or dulness, conceit, or immaturity in the critic has overlaid and depraved so many editions of the greatest poet of the world.

Horne Tooke spoke but the truth, when he said, " it is much to be wished that an edition of Shakespeare were given literatim according to the first Folio ; which is now become so scarce and dear that few persons can obtain it. For by the presumptuous license of the dwarfish commentators, who are for ever cutting him down to their own size, we risque the loss of Shakespeare's genuine text; which that Folio assuredly contains; notwithstanding some slight errors of the press which might be noted without altering." Diversions of Purley, ed. 1798, Vol. 2. p. 52.

Forestalling a remark to have been made in due course, and with a view to support this charge of Horne Tooke's against the commentators; to push it to the minutest particulars; to prove that they either find, or make a flaw in the clearest and most perfect sentence, a passage shall be here quoted from "Measure for Measure," a play unpublished in Quarto, but not more noticeable for the evident accuracy with which it has been handed down to us in the Folio, than for the strange, and manifold mistakes, committed by subsequent editors and glossarists in their treatment of it.

In Act 3. Sc. 1, Claudio says to his sister,

> "Why giue you me this shame?
> Thinke you I can a resolution fetch
> From floweric tendernesse? If I must die,
> I will encounter darknesse as a bride,
> And hugge it in mine armes."

This speech of Claudio is so pointed in the Folio, so by Mr. Halliwell, so by the Cambridge editors, (with a note that in his edition of 1857 a full stop is substituted for the mark of interrogation at " tenderness" by Dyce after Heath), and so by Mr. Dyce in his edition now in progress. Mr. Halliwell, adopting Capell's explanation, says, the meaning is, " Why do you thus put me to shame? Think you my resolution is to be formed by eloquent pathos? Claudio is now indignant that his sister should imagine he had not courage to prepare for death without being reasoned into it. This interpretation seems more natural than Heath's, " I must desire that you, on your part, will do me the justice to think that I am able to draw a resolution from this tenderness of my youth, which is commonly found to be less easily reconciled to so sudden and so harsh a fate.'" So far Halliwell; and fair fall the wit that finds " flowery tenderness" in Isabel's reasoning; or thinks to cloak a transparent repugnancy between the two, under the appellation, " eloquent pathos;" as if that were as warranted a synonym for the one, as it may pass for a tolerable description of the other; nor sees withal how absurd it would be in Claudio to emulate the pathos that he decries: but happiest head of all be his dole, that by altering a point, with Heath, can treat "flowery tenderness" as the usual attribute of manhood, and conceive the fetching thence a resolution to die to be a feat either natural or suitable. The same mind that could characterise Claudio's age and sex by flowery tenderness, is not such as would extract from it the courage to meet an untimely and a shameful death. How Mr. Dyce interprets the passage can only be surmised; the punctuation of Heminge and Condell, which in his first edition was dislodged by Heath's, is reinstated in his second, his present edition, but it may be again over-ruled in his " Addenda ;" for there is an odd mixture of positiveness and vacillation in his comments, venial in greener heads, that is very mortifying to such, and they are not few in number, who entertain the highest respect for his plain sense and undoubted scholarship. However, you may boldly say that not an editor or annotator of them all has apprehended the poet's meaning: certainly this has not been done by either Heath or Capell: and had the right key to it, a sufficiently obvious one, been known to others, the true purport of Claudio's words would not be given for the first time now.

" Flowery tenderness" was rightly understood by preceding expositors to be a figurative expression, but they missed to recognise in it an abstract for woman, her loveliest and most native, her first best quality. As with the ancients, a point by and by to be noticed, " masculine virtue," we are told,* is personated by the man Perseus, so with us moderns, and namely here in Shakespeare, by " flowery tenderness" woman is expressed. Out of some dozen apposite places that establish this—one,—but such a one as once to have seen, much more to have edited their works where it is found, forbids the thought that it could ever be forgot: the sentiment is itself so just, and the handling of it so exquisitely characteristic of the writers. In Act 5. Sc. 2. of Beaumont and Fletcher's "Thierry and Theodoret," Thierry says to his mother,

* Jonson's Masque of Queens.

12

> " Oh mother, do not lose your name, forget not
> The touch of nature in you, tenderness,
> 'Tis all the soul of woman, all the sweetness."

After the high Roman fashion Isabel lectures her
brother about death, and obtrudes her fears of his
courage to meet it ; whereupon poor Claudio naturally
enough resents this imputation upon his manhood, and
disdains to be beholden to his sister, to a woman, to
" flowery tenderness" for a resolution to die ; out-
bidding withal the tone of superiority assumed by the
weaker sex in an extravagant boast, soon to be falsified,
that he would " encounter darkness as a bride, and
hug it in his arms."

How finely are the austere precepts, the brave ad-
monitions of a maiden that wished "a more strict
restraint upon the sisterhood, the votarists of St.
Clare," contrasted by the poet with Juliet's timid and
sensitive apostrophe to the " injurious love," which
respites a sentenced criminal for a few hours from
execution, to spend the interim, as Spenser has it,
" half dead with dying fear," a life so punctually
limited, that in Shakespeare's nicer reckoning, its pro-
longation, which is " its very comfort," was " still a
dying horror" !

Here again we have lighted upon a second passage
now for the first time explained aright. It is a
crucial instance, and from among two or three more
in the same play, such as affords a delicate test for
discriminating between the reader who is at home in
Shakespeare's English, and one that has studied it

but as a strange tongue. The sense is utterly missed by every editor and commentator, early or late, learned or unlearned, who has essayed to give it. Hanmer first corrupted the text, and that is the sum of his success. Mason and Dyce applaud and adopt his corruption with a like result. They are as wide of the true meaning as Johnson, and Steevens, and Tollet, and Halliwell. What Shakespeare wrote and what Heminge and Condell printed, now to a tittle reprinted by Mr. Staunton, is this:—

> *Duke.*—" There rest :
> Your partner (as I heare) must die to morrow
> And I am going with instruction to him,
> Grace goe with you, *Benedicite.*   [*Exit.*
> *Jul.*—Must die to morrow? O injurious Loue
> That respits me a life, whose very comfort
> Is still a dying horror.
> *Pro.*—'Tis pitty of him."   [*Exeunt.*

Mr. Dyce's note is as follows: "The folio has ' *Oh injurious Loue,*'—well does Mason observe that both Johnson's explanation of this passage (with the old reading) and Steevens' refutation of it prove the necessity of Hanmer's amendment (law), which removes every difficulty, and can scarce be considered as an alteration, the trace of the letters in the words *law* and *love* being so nearly alike—the law affected the life of the man only" (referring to Johnson's hypothesis that Juliet's life was respited on account of her pregnancy) " not that of the woman : and this is the injury that Juliet complains of, as she wished to die with him." It will be seen that neither Mason nor Dyce accounts for the words "a life whose very comfort is still a dying horror," nor for the Provost's reply, " 'tis pity of him." The replacement of " love" by " law" might be justified by similarity of letters, but the obstacles to their exposition of the text thus vitiated are left as insurmountable as before.

The Cambridge editors and Mr. Halliwell retain the authentic reading " love," the former without comment, the latter interpreting thus: " Love here as in other instances is merely used in the sense of kindness. ' Injurious love' is nearly equivalent to the very common phrase, mistaken kindness." So far not amiss; although more nearly synonymous with " injurious love" would be " cruel kindness," words by which, with yet graver meaning, the *Times* in a leader of the 5th of November '64, reflected public opinion of the attempt of certain Germans to save a murderer from the gallows. But Mr. Halliwell goes on: " O injurious kindness which spares my life, a burden to me worse than death, whose very comfort in the love of Claudio is still a dying horror. 'Tis pity of him, that is of Angelo, that he should be so severe." Whatever be the meaning of this cloudy paraphrase—the text is sunlight to it—Mr. Halliwell, in common with the rest, understands the respited life to be Juliet's; he is however singular in endeavouring to reconcile the Provost's reply, " 'Tis pity of him," with Juliet's alleged bewailment of her own hard lot; and is entitled to credit for confronting a difficulty, which has not been faced, perhaps not observed by any but him: he is likely to be as singular in the twist which he gives to the Provost's words, and in applying them to Angelo.

Had Juliet's reflection not been intelligible in itself, the Provost's answer would convict the editors and commentators of inexcusable blundering. Let jocular Grumio catch at the ambiguity in his master's bidding, "Knock me here soundly,"* to make Petruchio the subject of the knocking meant by him for the gate, but let not a grave bench of Aristarchuses enforce Grumio's syntax elsewhere, to the marring of the sense, with its usual accompaniment, disturbance of the text. Petruchio's "me" in "knock me here soundly," and Juliet's "me" in "respites me a life," bear just the same import. It is a very hackneyed mode of speaking, not peculiar to the English language, used both in prose and verse, either in light or serious discourse.

And here one cannot but remark how preposterous is that system of education which instructs a boy in the usage of a Greek pronoun, and leaves him at ripe age, and even to grey hairs, insensible of a precisely similar use of the same pronoun in English; which teaches him at sixteen to construe readily from a Greek Play such an instance as occurs for example in the second line of Sophocles' Œdipus Tyrannus,† and finds him at sixty, in a parallel

---

* "The Taming of the Shrew," Act I. Sc. 2.

† Τίνας ποθ' ἕδρας τάσδε μοι θοάζετε;

instance from Shakespeare, so completely at fault about the words "respites me a life," as to be driven to maintain that an unrivalled dramatist, a bard of bards, had represented a young lady, whose life the law could not be said so much to spare, as not to touch at all, one who was to "live the lease of nature, and pay her breath to time and mortal custom," who might survive her speech for half a century, speaking of that life as "respited," and its "very comfort" throughout fifty years to come, as "still a dying horror"! "Cowards, indeed, die many times before their deaths," but even their life is not a life-long horror of dying, not a life-long death-pang. The sum is this,—"must die to-morrow,"— the Friar's tidings reiterated by Juliet, words under which lie couched the painful suspense of death, the poise and lingering descent of the executioner's uplifted axe, those few but pregnant words are the thesis to which her after discourse is wholly confined, and every syllable of that discourse would be as true and just in the mouth of the Provost, or of a commentator, as in Juliet's: what prompted the utterance of it was a "fee grief due to her single breast," her lover's death the next day: of that grief as the Provost's answer, "'tis pity of him," is the appropriate acknowledgment, so is it incompatible with any other version of her speech than that given above.

But to return whence was digressed. Granted that one or two Quartos furnish better readings in a few instances than the Folio; granted that they contain passages omitted in that edition which we should be sorry to lose, or which may be wanted to fill up a gap in the sense; granted that the wording and sentiments of the author's MS. were not scrupulously retained in the Play-house copies, or that both have in the Folio here and there undergone a little " Buttering ;" one of which last things, unless Ben Jonson be not only inaccurate but untruthful, must have happened in the case of the passage from Julius Cæsar, ridiculed in his " Staple of News," and again formally censured in his " Discoveries;" granted also that such misprints as that of " *clamour*" for " chamber your tongues," in the Winter's Tale, which supplied Taylor the Water-Poet with a scrap of verbose nonsense,* may be far from solitary, yet is Horne Tooke's assertion still true, that " it is much to be wished that an edition of Shakespeare were given literatim according to the first Folio."

A ready means of testing the soundness of this position may now be had: let the reader contrast Mr. Howard Staunton's edition of Shakespeare, or indeed any other,† with what, under that gentleman's supervision, is already reprinted by Day, and reprinted with unerring accuracy, from the edition by Heminge and Condell: of the verdict of the English scholar

---

* " Sir Gregory Nonsense his Newes from Noplace." Taylor's Workes, Ed. 1630, p. 1.

† The comparative accuracy of recent reprints of the 1st Folio forms no part of the question.

there cannot be a doubt. Nothing could surpass this reprint but what we have not got, and are not likely to have, a text selected with judgement from the earliest Quartos, and first Folio; their various readings given at foot, as well as the rare amendments, and passing rare they are, from later editions.

Horne Tooke inveighs against the dwarfish commentators of his time, but they are giants beside the punies of ours. Then increased acquaintance with the idioms of Shakespeare's day tended to uphold the original text, where now a more discursive, but superficial, ill-digested reading seems prone to blemish and unsettle it. With one or two distinguished exceptions, and those not always true to themselves, the modern explorers of Shakespeare's text, finding in it much that is to them uncouth both in thought and expression, love better to tax their ingenuity in guessing what he should have written by what they can apprehend, than to search painfully for what he meant by what he did write. Poeta nascitur non fit, is verified also of the critic: for one that is at the pains to qualify himself by research to interpret, a score undertake on one foot to re-write Shakespeare, and it is hard to determine whether the enterprise or its success is more to be admired. To correct Magnificat, and teach Shakespeare how to fashion his speech, have both one disease; and if the intensity of the disease may be gathered from the spread and aggravation of the symptoms, things are becoming worse and worse. Time was when Zachary Jackson appeared like an owl at mid-day, a sight to be wondered at; now he is in some repute, and has a host of copyists—indeed the Cambridge editors pronounce " the judgment of the Author of 'Shakespeare's genius justified' worth all consideration," and accordingly make up their hotchpot of various readings from trash of his, and of his copesmate, Andrew Beckett, the rank folly whereof disedges all relish for the tooth-some Quarto and Folio collation, set before their guests in such ill neighbourhood. To patronise quacksalvers like them, and record their nostrums, belongs not to the masculine duty of an editor of Shakespeare, but savours strongly of the office assigned by Iago to his pattern woman, " to suckle fools and chronicle small beer." Simple vain Zachary loved his own barn better than Shakespeare's house; the smoke of his conceited noddle was pleasanter to his eyes than the clearest fire of his author's intellect. So it fares with all the sort of them: professing to reverence the memory of Shakespeare, they violate his remains; the monument reared by his own genius they chip and deface, they plaster and daub, or in Zachary's phrase " they justify," and to get themselves a men-tion, they bescribble it all over with their names. The Cambridge editors appear to spare no pains to propagate this vainglorious itch; every additional volume brings its additional Jackson or Beckett. Nor is this prurient meddlesomeness, this hankering after notoriety confined to the illiterate rout, who subject the grey authority of the Folio to their childish alphabetical quirks; whose sole materials of

criticism are syllable and sound; their only organs
of judgement, the eye and the ear; which shuffle
'gnat' into 'quat,' 'part' into 'dart,' 'broom' into
'brown,' 'degrees' into 'diseases,' 'Jupiter' into
'pulpiter;' empirics, whose acquaintance with an
author does not so much as embrace the evidence
supplied by his repeating and expounding of himself:
no, its taint has infected those who have proceeded
masters of their art, who, if they do not always,
when they might, illustrate Shakespeare by Shakespeare, have yet for that purpose ransacked chap-books
and broad-sheets, have scoured the by-ways and
dark corners of contemporary literature, have served
a lifelong apprenticeship to the subject, and both
with their own countrymen and with foreigners are
its recognised oracles.

Expende Hannibalem—put Mr. Collier into the
scales; say what weight is to be attached to his
appraisement of a suspected reading, that can garnish
an edition of Shakespeare, the consummate product
of his maturest studies, with notes of this stamp?
In Vol. 1. p. [265, he says of the Merchant of Venice
—" there is a remarkable proof of its popularity in
the work of a rival dramatist, Webster; it is in his
" White Devil," (printed in 1612, but when first
acted is uncertain), where Vittoria, on her trial, makes
a reference to the heroine of Shakespeare's " Merchant of Venice," and complains that she is

" So intangled in a cursed accusation,
That my defence, of force, like Portia's,
Must personate masculine virtue."

In the original editions Portia's is misprinted Perseus, but the Rev. Mr. Mitford suggested the excellent emendation, which the Rev. Mr. Dyce (i. p. 65) was too timid to adopt, though he had the courage to print nonsense."

It is Mr. Collier's hard lot never to display less erudition, or worse judgement, than when he is most peremptory and magisterial. To this suicidal attack upon him Mr. Dyce rejoins, " Mr. Mitford's conjecture, though Mr. Collier pronounces it "excellent," I believe to be unquestionably wrong. Apart from the extreme improbability that Webster would make Vittoria allude to a character in the Merchant of Venice—the passage itself shows that neither Shakespeare's Portia, nor (as I suggested in my second ed. of Webster) Portia, the wife of Brutus, is the person in question. Whoever that personage may have been, she like Vittoria had to offer a " defence against some heavy accusation" under which she laboured— as to the expression " masculine virtue" I may notice that Heywood in the Fifth Book of his Various Historic concernynge Women, p. 224. ed. 1624, treats " of warlike women and those of masculine virtue," but nothing is found there which throws any light on the speech of Vittoria."

Mr. Dyce may, according to Mr. Collier, have " had the courage to print nonsense," but sense or nonsense, he printed what Webster wrote ; and though Mr. Mitford prefer Portia's to Perseus, and Mr. Collier dub it an "excellent emendation," yet since

Mr. Dyce undertook to edit Webster, not Mitford or Collier, and since Webster might not care to father Mitford and Collier's excellent emendation, as being of the mind that "a civil doctor" is not the fittest type of masculine virtue, Webster's readers, if he have any, should be left in undisturbed possession of what Webster wrote. Mr. Collier, among those qui novo marmori ascribunt Praxitelem suo, can manufacture and antedate a thousand new readings in Shakespeare, if such be his humour; and his readings may pass muster with Professor Mommsen, and the rest, who like Shakespeare accommodated to modern parlance, or recast in the grotesque mould of a Jackson or a Beckett. He can also, for lack of better, suborn evidence of the popularity of Shakespeare's Merchant of Venice out of Mr. Mitford's corruption of Webster's text, but he cannot avoid the proof that Webster wrote Perseus not Portia's. Let the reader turn to Jonson's "Masque of Queens celebrated from the house of fame by the Queen of Great Britain with her ladies at Whitehall, Feb. 2. 1609," three years before Webster's White Devil was printed, and he will find in it what Webster found before him, how "a person by this time descended in the furniture of Perseus, and expressing heroic and masculine virtue began to speak," with a note by the author that "the ancients expressed a brave and masculine virtue in three figures (of Hercules, Perseus, and Bellerophon) of which," adds he, "we choose that of Perseus armed as we have described him out of Hesiod, Scut. Here. See Apollodorus the grammarian, liber 2. de Perseo."

Webster's allusion may be far-fetched, and its wording somewhat queer, but otherwise where is the difficulty? Vittoria excuses herself for being forced to lay aside modesty and womanhood, and represents that in her defence she has been driven to set forth, like Perseus, the language and bearing of masculine virtue; in plain words, she says that she must conduct her defence with the rough vigour of a man (Perseus, not Bellario being her model) instead of the bashful weakness of a woman. The inference suggested by this dispute about Perseus appears to be, that one may edit Shakespeare twice without having read Ben Jonson once. And indeed his gratuitous discovery of the imperfect knowledge possessed by him of the works of Beaumont and Fletcher, of Shirley, and Middleton, as well as of Ben Jonson, abundantly proclaims Mr. Collier's peculiar qualifications for his accomplished work, the disfigurement of Shakespeare. At p. 67 of Vol. 1. in a note on a line from Act 4. Sc. 1. of the Tempest, criticising Mr. Dyce's edition of Middleton's " Spanish Gipsy," he affirms in his dictatorial way—" on p. 196. ' rage' of the old copies ought to be ' rags,' " to which Mr. Dyce successfully retorts—" as to ' age' which I substituted for ' rage' of the old copies—

Alv.   " I could wish
For one hour's space I could pluck back from time
But thirty years, that in my fall

> Thou might'st deserve report : now if thou conquer'st
> Thou canst not triumph, I'm half dead already
> Yet I'll not start a foot.
> *Louis.*—Breathes there a spirit
> In such a heap of age?"

The alteration is one of several important changes made with a pen in my copy of the first 4to by some early possessor, who, as he has also inserted additions to the text, had in all probability seen a manuscript of the play. The edition of 1816, like Mr. Collier, altered "rage" to "rags;" but see the context; and compare in "The Old Law" by Massinger, Middleton, and Rowley

> "Take hence that pile of years."
>
> Act 2. Sc. 1."

The context alone puts Mr. Collier's reading out of court, but his evil genius betrayed him to shew that he had overlooked, or forgotten, or never read to any purpose Beaumont and Fletcher's "Maid's Tragedy," where, in Act 1. Sc. 2, the context is quite as tolerant of "rags," as in Middleton's "Spanish Gipsy," although "age" is not there misprinted "rage."

> *Melantius.*—"That heap of age which I should reverence
> If it were temperate ; but testy years
> Are most contemptible."

The like may be observed of Shirley's "School of Complement." Act 3. Sc. 1.

> *Selina.*—"Whither had reason so withdrawn itself
> I could not make distinction of a man
> From such a heap of age, aches, and rheum?"

Mr. Collier's rage for rags has led him to give

"rags" for "rage" ("rebellion—guarded with rage") in Act 4. Sc. 1, of the 2nd part of K. Henry 4th, where, though he have Mr. Sidney Walker, Mr. Dyce, the Cambridge editors, and all the rest to abet him (Mr. Halliwell excepted) it will hereafter be shown that Heminge and Condell's text is without "brack," and not to be mended by "rags."

It is not however of his country's speech as employed in the writings of her dramatists alone, but universally, in what way soever transmitted, that Mr. Collier's knowledge is defective; and he is so amusingly unconscious of it that he does not flinch from thrusting out of Shakespeare words met with every where besides, and introducing in their room others of his own coinage, or the refuse of some previous commentator. Thus in " Measure for Measure," Act 5. Sc. 1, the Folio gives

" Make rash remonstrance of my hidden power."

" Unquestionably the printer's error," says Mr. Collier, " for ' demonstrance': he used the wrong preposition. Shakespeare elsewhere has ' demonstration' and ' demonstrate,' but this is the only place where demonstrance occurs." It is so; the only place; and Mr. Collier put it there, having borrowed it from Malone's remark—" As I am not aware of remonstrance being used in this sense I would read demonstrance." But though Malone knew no other instance, both he, and his editor, Boswell, kept the authentic word in the text: to drive it thence was reserved for Mr. Collier, who did know one. For just as Shakespeare does here, so does Shirley in his "Hyde Park" use "remonstrance"—"another misprint for demonstrance," ingeminates Mr. Collier, "the same carelessness of the old compositor as to the preposition having caused the error in both instances." But in Act 1. Sc. 2. of "The Imposture" by the same dramatist, as Mr. Dyce insists, the word is found again with a like meaning. Now would it not be marvellous if but thrice over "the carelessness of the old compositor as to the preposition" had, for a counterfeit of Malone's, caused the misprint of a sterling and current word; correctly stated by Mr. Grant White "to have come only comparatively of late years to mean expostulation"? Mr. Halliwell observes, "Remonstrance seems to be used here in a peculiar sense of show or discovery from the Latin 'monstro.'" Mr. Dyce relates that Gifford pronounces the word in this sense "catachrestic" (an epithet more applicable to half the words in our language) and that Walker asks, may not the word have been in use in the sense of "exhibition"? Behold, so probable to thinking is the use, that a mere metre-monger, dismounted from his hobby, can divine, and very little search, as will be seen, is needed to ascertain it.

How often, when his own reading does not bestead him, would recourse to his Dictionary spare many a commentator much idle speculation, even to the making what erewhile seemed extraordinary, or recondite, surprisingly common-place, and apparent!

And mark how Shakespeare's true text is needlessly bandied to and fro by neglect of this vicarious and cheap expedient. In 1859 Mr. Staunton edits "Measure for Measure," with "demonstrance" in the text, pursuant to Malone's suggestion and Collier's example; in 1863 the Cambridge editors register Mr. Staunton as the first to have made this change, (erroneously, that dull eminence was pre-occupied by Mr. Collier); in 1864 Mr. Staunton in a second edition replaces the original word, with the somewhat disingenuous foot-note: "So the old text, and rightly, though Malone and other writers persist in reading remonstrance." It is plain then that Malone's castaway was adopted both by Mr. Collier and Mr. Staunton; the one proud to father, the other now eager to disclaim all partnership in the foundling. But thus do orts and leavings of past editors become the main stock of present ones; and texts of the Folio which have run the gauntlet of more skilled judgements are held fit material on which to try the prentice hand. Both Johnson and Richardson adduce examples of the noun "remonstrance" in the not very abusive, nor yet uncommon sense of manifestation, or declaration. These being easily accessible need not be repeated here, but a few more shall be added for the sake of the insight they afford into the literary endowments, which, by popular allowance, license a scholiast or editor of Shakespeare to cashier the old text.

In the "Divil's Charter," by Barnabe Barnes, 1607, the Duke of Candy says,

"Those (warres) are the same they seeme, and in such warres
Your sonne shall make remonstrance of his valour,
And so become true champion of the Church."

ACT I. Sc. 4. Sig. B. 3.

In "The Lost Lady," 1639, the "Physitian" says,

"makes his escape, and is received
Of the Spartana king with all remonstrances
Of love, and confess'd service."—P. 4.

In Taylor's Sermons, 1653-4, we find

"They that perished in the gainsaying of Corah were out of the condition of repentance ; but the people that were affrighted with the neighbourhood of the judgement, and the expresses of God's anger manifested in such visible remonstrances, they were the men called to repentance."—Page 162. Serm. 13. Part 2.

In South's Posthumous Sermons, ed. 1744, we encounter

"No : the atheist is too wise in his generation to make remonstrances and declarations of what he thinks."—Serm. 3. p. 78. Vol. 9.

Whatever be the authority of Barnes or Barclay, it cannot be denied that Taylor and South are good bail for Shakespeare's use of "remonstrance," though to Malone it be unexampled, to Gifford catachrestic, and to Halliwell peculiar. Neither must it be supposed that remonstrance is some abnormal birth, uncountenanced by other members of its family. Both Johnson and Richardson give instances of the verb, signifying to manifest, or declare ; and in Act 5. Sc. 2. of Jonson's "Every Man out of his Humour,"

Amorphus says, " Lo, you have given yourself the
dor. But I will remonstrate to you the third dor,
which is not as the two former dors, indicative but
deliberative." So also Jeremy Taylor, " I did
insist the longer upon this instance that I might
remonstrate how great and how sure and how pre-
serving (misprint for persevering) mercies a pious
father of a family may derive upon his succeeding
generations." Page 47. Serm. 4. Part 2. And
again, " In order to which end my purpose now is
to remonstrate to you the several states of sin and
death together with those remedies which God had
proportioned out to them.' Page 199. Serm. 16.
Part 1. We likewise find it in the translation of
Rabelais by Urquhart and Motteux. Book 3. chap.
34 : " to tell them in downright terms and to remonstrate to them (orig. remonstrant), with a great show
of detestation of a crime so horrid, how their hus-
bands were jealous." At page 116 of the English
Mirrour, by George Whetstones, 1586, we meet
with " remonstration," and at page 12 of " Death's
Sermon unto the Living," by Charles Fitz-Geffry,
1662, we meet with " remonstrable," " thus you see
the Doctrine is for evidence most remonstrable."

If then Horace's rule hold good, enough, and more
than enough, has been alleged to vindicate Shakespeare, Heminge and Condell, Jaggard, and the old
compositor, and to negative Gifford's charge of
catachresis, as well as Halliwell's notion of pecu-
liarity. But to sift the subject to the bottom, ab-

solutely to justify this employment of the word remonstrance, to shew that it is genuine and proper, as
well as that it was customary and received, it may
be asked; is there any solecism in the composition
of the verbs "revere" or "resolve"? or will it be
said that "recommend" and "recompense" are open
to objection, because classical Latin knows no such
compounds as "recommendo" or "recompenso"? On
the same ground is there catachresis in "revestry"
or "regreet"? Cannot an actuary in casting accounts "rebate," or when hungry take his "repast,"
and speak so too, without abuse of speech? Gifford
would not and Mr. Collier cannot deny that "renie"
and "renege" were once in use, ("denege" never),
where now, "renegade" excepted, forms with the
prefix 'de' are only prevalent. And it is worthy of
remark that although Vossius devotes two chapters,
the 20th and 21st in his 4th book de vitiis sermonis,
to compounds of 're,' wherein he affirms "Renego
pro nego, denego plane culpandum;" yet, whether
from oversight or not, he makes no mention of "re-
monstro," a compound as little occurring in good
Latin as "renego," but in middle and low Latin by
no means hard to meet with. Besides the passages
cited by Du Cange under the words "Remonstrantia"
and "Remonstrare" take the two following: In a
note, Book 2. chap. 6. of Rabelais by Urquhart and
Motteux, explaining why the Limosins are called
turnip-eaters, the gloss quotes John Hotman as reporting of them, that " cum audirent quod papa erat

vicarius Dei, immo quod ipsemet erat Deus (ut patet
per canonistas) miserunt sibi legationem ad remon-
strandam paupertatem patriæ suæ, in qua fere nihil
crescit præter rapas et castaneas." And in Part 3.
Sec. 2. Memb. 2. Subs. 1. of Burton's Anatomy of
Melancholy, he has in a note "Tho. Campanella
Astrologiæ, lib. 4. cap. 8. articulis 4 and 5 insaniam
amatoriam remonstrantia multa præ cæteris accumu-
lat aphorismata."

And now, if it were not an ungracious office to
lecture a patriarch pupil, and bid him new-learn his
lesson, notwithstanding the entire league between
formal ignorance and grave obstinacy one might
fairly call upon Mr. Collier to do "the old compositor" right by undoing the wrong which in this
instance at all events, unless he would put out his
own, as well as other people's eyes, he must know
that the Queen's English has sustained at his hands.
That gentleman's Shakespeare is not specially under
review, but the labour of a life devoted to the task,
and the manner in which it has at last been exe-
cuted by him, warrant the prominence given to its
blots in these introductory remarks; of which one
design is to exhibit the degeneracy of the existing
breed of expositors. Among the comments of those
who ranked highest in an older and abler race nothing
like the blemishes, thick strewn throughout Mr.
Collier's last edition, nothing simile aut secundum is
anywhere to be found. The names of Theobald,
Steevens, and Malone would have slept in the same

grave, to which their coevals and posterity have
justly consigned the memories of Jackson and
Beckett, had they wrought no better for the elucida-
tion of Shakespeare, and therewithal for the rescue
of good English from the mongrel character which
conceit and ignorance are ever bent to impress upon
it. To clear up an obscurity the approved practice
was to borrow light from Shakespeare's time-fellows,
where none was reflected by himself, and not without more ado to proscribe every hard saying as
spurious; or to assume a misprint, jostle out the old
reading, and foist into its place whatever Hob or
Dick may judge fittest. Day by day we are more
and more receding from the phraseology of Shakespeare's age, and so new difficulties are daily raised,
new changes in the text proposed to meet the usage
of the hour; with these has grown up, if they have
not given rise to it, a taste for cavilling and cobbling,
nicknamed acute and felicitous, but in truth the poor
make-believe of a shallow unlettered criticism: to
this taste Mr. Collier has catered, in his last edition
of Shakespeare, with a prodigality by so much more
censurable, as it is more mischievous, than the slavish
adherence to the old copies, which for the most part
marked his first. He has reversed the characteristics
of life's gradation. ("degrees," one dare not say for
one's head, because of its affinity, both in letters and
sound, to "diseases." K. Henry 4th. Part 2. Act. 1.
Sc. 2.) In him the caution of youth has been suc-
ceeded by the rashness of age; the once crabbed

textuary, that was wont to blanch the most glaring
misprints, is now become the licentious innovator to
brand the sincerest readings. It is then of Mr.
Collier, as the representative and ringleader of a
school injurious to Shakespeare, to the old drama,
and to the integrity of the English language, that
this notice has been taken; it is because his authority
has exercised a contagious influence upon minds that
should have been proof against its working; because, as shall be forthwith indicated, an editor of
Shakespeare, qualified above all others for the office,
has not escaped its blight.

Appositely enough, as some no doubt will think,
the case exhibiting an instance of this, and which we
are now about to canvass, is from " Much ado about
Nothing:" though the statement be somewhat prolix,
the reader will be in fault if it does not prove in-
structive also. In Act 5. Sc. 1. of that play, according to the Quarto (1600), and the Folio, we
read—

" Scambling, outfacing, fashion-monging boys."

In the 2nd, 3rd and 4th Folios, three in number,
but one in effect, each faultier than its predecessor,
and none of any authority, as likewise in all the
modern editions down to Mr. Knight's, " fashion-
monging" becomes " fashion-mong'ring." It is not
a matter of any importance which mode of spelling
may be adopted, so far as the sense is concerned, but
Shakespeare being in the hands and on the lips of all,

upon his writings, next to our version of the Bible,
and to the book of Common Prayer, depend the per-
petuation of old, and the defence of calumniated English. What avails it that "monging" is found in
the "Funeralles of King Edward the Syxt," 1560.

> "Your monging of vitayles, corne, butter and cheese."

In the "Coblers Prophesie," 1594.

> "And the money monging mate with all his knaverie."—
>
> Sig. **B. 3.**

In Lord Brooke's "Treatise of Religion," composed
many years before, but first printed in 1670.

> "Book learning, arts, yea school divinity
> New types of old law-monging Pharisies."—Stanza 67.

In Gee's "New Shreds of the Old Snare," 1624.
" But the Pope's benediction, or any the least touch
of sainting, miracle-monging fiction is able to in-
fuse the highest worth into the basest baggagely new-
nothing to hang upon the sleeve of admiring, adoring,
ghostly children of the Jesuites."—Pp. 49-50. What
avail these, or any number of like instances, buried
in writers that are never read? Banish the true and
genuine form "monging" from Shakespeare, it becomes an outcast from our language, and leaves a
gap in the eldest branch of a most useful family of
words.

" Monging" is the present participle regularly in-
flected from the Anglo-Saxon verb 'mangian' to
traffick : in the example cited above from Baldwin
it is the very same word as "mangung," merchandise.
Again from the verb mangian we get "monger,"

now used only in composition, but in Shakespeare's time occurring as a simple noun, *e.g.* in Ben Jonson's " Tale of a Tub."

> *Hilts.* " Here was no subtle device to get a wench!
> This chanon has a brave pate of his own,
> A shaven pate, and a right monger y'vaith."
>
> Act 2. Se. 1.

In Philemon Holland's translation of " Plinies Naturall History," 1600. " Againe it falleth out that sometime one rich munger or other (praevalens manceps) buying up a commoditie, and bringing it wholly into his owne hands for to have the monopolie of it raiseth the market and enhaunceth the price."—Book 33, p. 485. Notwithstanding these examples, and no doubt others might be adduced, the separate subsistence of " monger" will be found on reference to our Grammarians and Lexicographers to be denied by some, and questioned by most of them. Within twenty years after Holland's translation, the learned but crotchety master of St. Paul's School, Alexander Gil, in the chapter on compounds of his " Logonomia Anglica," ed. 1619, says, "munger inseparabile est & illum denotat qui rem venalem habet ut fishmunger, cetarius." Somner attaches some sort of authority to this idle assertion. Lye calls the word old English still found in composition. Johnson cautiously says " monger is seldom or never used alone," while Todd quotes the passage from the " Tale of a Tub," and adds that " Wicliffe, he thinks, uses it somewhere in the good sense of a trader."

c 2

As to "mongering," that form also is quite legitimate, being the present participle of "mangheren," termed by Kilian an old low Dutch word; but why should an inflection from the more elementary and indigenous root be shouldered out by one from what is in all likelihood but an offshoot from it?

In justice to the several annotators and editors of Shakespeare it is desirable, however tiresome, that their comments should be set before the reader. Malone notices indeed that the "old copies,"—meaning the Quarto and Folio, for he was too sagacious so to designate the three Folio republications that followed—read "monging," yet he put mong'ring in his text: to Mr Knight is due the credit of restoring the true form, with this brief and sensible note— "Fashion-monging," so the original copies; but always altered to fashion-mong'ring. The participle of the Anglo-Saxon verb meaning to trade, would give us monging; as the verb gives us the noun signifying a trader—"monger." Vol. 2. p. 444. He is followed by Mr. Halliwell, with a note to the same effect, and by the Cambridge editors, who, with their usual fidelity, the highest praise of their work, ascribe " monging" to the Quarto and Folio, " mongering" to the three subsequent editions. Mr. Collier's is a pattern note; the whole piece, his edition of 1856, for spirit, veracity, and scholarship, sorts with it. "The Rev. A. Dyce," says he, "in his 'Few notes,' &c. p. 46, would have this compound spelt 'fashion-monging,' merely because he so finds it in Wilson's

' Cobler's Prophecie,' 1594. This is to desert the
etymology of the word ; and the same reason would
require adherence to every old and exploded form in
any other word. In Wilson's comedy we may be
pretty sure that the letter ' r' in mong'ring was ac-
cidentally omitted." Vol. 2. p. 71. Upon this note
of Mr. Collier's the subjoined comment is made by
Mr. Dyce in his edition now in progress. " In my
Few Notes, &c., p. 46, I have said, " Here Mr. Knight
alone of the modern editors follows the old copies in
printing fashion-monging—and rightly, &c. : but now
in considering the inconsistency in spelling which those
old copies exhibit, I think that the other modern
editors have done more wisely. Mr. Collier in the
second edition of his Shakespeare writes thus on the
present passage—(see above)—one of Mr. Collier's
many unprincipled attempts to render me ridiculous
in the eyes of his readers ; few of whom could be
expected to know (what Mr. Collier could not fail to
know) that in the present passage all the old editions,
the quarto and the four folios (Mr. Dyce is mistaken
about the three last) are uniform in having " fashion-
monging." Vol. 2. p. 155. It is to be regretted
that Mr. Dyce should have vailed his first and sounder
judgement to Mr. Collier's worthless assertion ; it is
yet more to be regretted that either Mr. Collier, or
any one else, that thinks himself competent to edit
Shakespeare, should ever dream that even with the
credulous and illiterate his bare word will either
avouch or refute an etymology, or that his surmise

about letters dropt out, or prepositions mistook, will countervail manifold evidence that nothing of the kind has occurred.

Before commencing a detailed and orderly comparison of the four editions of Shakespeare now issuing from the Press, namely, the reprint of Heminge and Condell's by Staunton, Halliwell's, the Cambridge, and Dyce's, with others in highest repute, it only remains to make good what was affirmed, that in interpreting Shakespeare his readers seem to have lost the power to follow the same rules of construction as they observe when writing themselves, or interpreting what is written by each other. To exemplify this, we will take a particular but not a rare usage of the three propositions " in," " to," and " into," which have altogether caused more spilth of ink (for every drop has been wasted) than might suffice to comment Shakespeare from title-page to colophon.

Hard above all has been the fate of ' in'; let but Iago say that for soldiership his comrade Cassio is " a fellow almost damned in a fair wife"—that his qualifications for the post of lieutenant would be almost discreditable in a woman; let him add withal, as though on set purpose to preclude every chance of being misunderstood, that Cassio possesses no more strategic knowledge than " a spinster," when lo! a goodly troop of commentators, clerk and lay, bishop and bookseller, lawyer and antiquary, critic professional and critic amateur, home-born and outlandish, men who have read much, and men who have read nothing, swarm forth to bury this simple remark under a pile of notes, that from first to last contain not an inkling of its purport. The passage is well known, but it will be of service to bring it under the reader's eye.

> "(A fellow almost damn'd in a faire wife)
> That never set a squadron in the field,
> Nor the devision of a battle knowes
> More then a spinster."   *Othello*, Act 1. Sc. 2.

The words are to be taken circumscriptly, not sent gadding after Bianca, or no one knows who; their meaning must be sought and found within the compass of the line in which they stand. Had Shakespeare written "A fellow almost damned in a raw lad," the dullest brain could scarcely have missed the imputation that Cassio's military abilities would be almost disallowed, condemned as hardly up to the mark in an inexperienced boy : or had the words run, "a fellow almost damned in an old maid," then, though it might not be understood how an officer, after Iago's report, of Cassio's incapacity, should be almost damned in one of her sex and condition, she at any rate could not, like the "fair wife," have been discovered at Cyprus in a young courtezan. Or not altering a syllable, with only a slight change in their order, let us place the words thus ;

> "A fellow in a fair wife almost damned,"

by this disposition of them, the reader is pinned to their true construction: the alliance between Cassio and the fair wife is closer than the commentators suspected; they harp upon conjugal union, Iago speaks of virtual identity; they seek the coupling of two persons in wedlock, he contemplates an embodiment of the soldiership of the one in the condition of the other, and so incorporated he pronounces it to be "in a fair wife" almost reproveable; adding, in the same vein, that it was no better than might be found in "a spinster." To dwell on this point longer would be to upbraid the reader's understanding.

Although however its sense has lain hid, the authentic reading of Heminge and Condell maintains its ground, their "wife" having outfaced Hanmer's "phiz"—"a fellow almost damned in a fair phiz," and outlived Tyrwhitt's "life," so well spoken of by Steevens and Ritson, the "spinster" quite forgot. Mr. Grant White has indeed printed "wise" for "wife;" without any meaning, but solely because the long s and f are often confounded: thus does every one "play at loggats" with Shakespeare's remains.

Touching the next preposition "to," it has not been so unlucky; if it be a sore stumbling-block in that line of the Duke's address to Escalus, "But that to your sufficiency as your worth is able," still a general, albeit hazy conception of the sense has been arrived at: and notwithstanding its vitiation by some editors and its question by all, both the line itself, and the whole speech to which it belongs, may, if any other, be safely upheld to have

been recorded by Heminge and Condell precisely
as it was penned by Shakespeare: for no one text
can there be amassed such overpowering testimony:
it is thrust upon you from all sides; in Shakespeare
himself it is not wanting, and in writers both of
prose and verse, before, at, and after his time vol-
umes of proof may be had. Reserving it on account
of its length for another occasion, we shall conclude
with the case of the preposition " into," as it occurs
in Act 1. Sc. 2, of the "Tempest," thus given by
Heminge and Condell :—

> " Like one
> Who hauing into truth, by telling of it,
> Made such a synner of his memorie
> To credite his owne lie, he did belecue
> He was indeed the Duke."

Now it should be premised that the punctuation of
the Folio, like most books of its date, is faulty, and
not otherwise to be regarded than as it tends to
support, or at all events not to overthrow the sense:
to read " Good :" in the third line of this play, " Good :
speake to the mariners:" with the pause indicated
by a colon; or to read "For why?" in the 11th
verse of the 16th Psalm, and the 41st verse of the
105th Psalm (old version) as a question, though
printed with a mark of interrogation, whether sanc-
tioned or not by Cowper in his " John Gilpin," or by
Henderson's recitation of that ballad, betokens ignorance not only of the old capricious punctuation, but
of the significance of phrases in vulgarest use. On

the other hand, it sometimes happens that the pointing in the original copies preserves the sense, which modern editors have hopelessly stopped out. Take a notable example in " Measure for Measure," Act 4. Sc. 2. The Duke exhibits a letter to the Provost, and says, " The contents of this is the returne of the Duke ; you shall anon over-reade it at your pleasure : where you shall finde within these two daies, he will be heere. This is a thing that Angelo knowes not; for hee this very day receives letters of strange tenor, perchance of the Duke's death, perchance entering into some monasterie, but by chance nothing of what is writ." So Heminge and Condell, reprinted without variance of speck or dot, by Mr. Staunton. All modern editors point the concluding words thus— " but, by chance, nothing of what is writ;"—then having by their pointing extinguished the sense, some corrupt, all misinterpret the sentence. Hanmer, at Warburton's instance, and Warburton, interpolating the adverb, " here," print " here writ:" in his present edition Mr. Dyce follows them : Mr. Halliwell makes no addition to the old text beyond the fatal commas. So also the Cambridge editors. But Mr. Halliwell gives it a most portentous meaning : like Mr. Staunton, who having newly turned " prenzie" into " reverend" therein only keeps decorum, he makes out that " writ" is here " holy writ," and signifies "truth ;" because we say, to take for writ or gospel, i. e. take for true, therefore in this place, " nothing of what is writ," amounts to " nothing of what is true." So

that according to editors and commentators, past and
present, Shakespeare makes the Duke positively
affirm that Angelo knew not of his coming, that on
the contrary he had that very day received letters of
strange tenor, letters purposely designed to mislead
him ; and then in the same breath makes the Duke
allege that it was by chance Angelo did not know
" the truth," that it was by chance he did not know
the contents of the letter in his hand, which an-
nounced the Duke's return within two days. This is
to outbrave Shakespeare, not to expound him : this
is to put Shakespeare not only not to speak like
Shakespeare, but not even like one that knew his
own mind. Let the reader be assured Shakespeare
is justly chargeable with no such contradiction.
According to Heminge and Condell the Duke tells
the Provost that in Angelo's letters of strange tenor
everything is written conjecturally, perchance of the
Duke's death, perchance entering into some monastery,
" but by chance nothing of what is writ," i.e. except
as a matter of chance nothing of what is writ—
nothing of what is writ in the letters received by
Angelo is set down otherwise than uncertainly.

Here happily, as in other places not a few, is no
room for cogging in words to get a meaning, no room
for experimenting on resemblance of letters, or the
clink of syllables : your critic ocular and auricular
is baffled ; unable to ring his changes of " close"
into " glose," " remonstrance" into "demonstrance,"
" crime" into " grime," " a point" into " report,"

"sob" into "bob" or "fob" (a change at which all
Shakespeare's boys laughed in amazement), the verbal
pedlar is out of his element, groping in the darkness
which envelopes every one unfamiliar with such
constructions as do not survive in modern literature.

In the above example from " Measure for Measure" we have seen how, as Chaucer sings, " the
reader that pointeth ill, a good sentence may oft
spill ;" that in fact the sense has been lost by the addition of points absent in the Folio ; but its common
fault in punctuation is on the side of excess : such is
the case in the passage from the Tempest ; the line,
—" who having into truth, by telling of it," has a
comma too much ; for the construction is, " telling of
it into truth." There exists little or no difference of
opinion as to the general purport of the whole passage, which is understood to convey the same thought
as these words in South's 8th Sermon, p. 305. Vol. 2.
ed. 1697. " like those who by often repeating a lie
to others come at length to believe it themselves,"
or as expressed more at large, in Ford's Play, by
King Henry, touching the impostor Perkin War-
beck ;

> " The lesson prompted and well conn'd was moulded
> Into familiar dialogue, oft rehearsed,
> Till learnt by heart, 'tis now received for truth."
>
> Act 5. Sc. 2.

But though the sentiment be trivial, the vulgar
construction in this place—" a sinner into truth," for
a sinner against truth,—has never been parallelled,
and until that be done, no good reason can be given

why a different syntax, neither strained, nor infrequent, should not prevail.

Perhaps the ensuing extracts will help to facilitate the apprehension of words so joined as in—" telling of it into truth." " After a further quantity of useless butchery and carnage, and after the innumerable hospitals have been some more times filled and emptied, this truth will grow into a familiar fact, and the next thing then necessary will be to have ready prepared some feasible line of frontier which may also be *discussed into familiarity.*"—The *Times*, Oct. 10, 1862. " Why thus also it is with the mind of man: after he is offended, if he will not be brought to discharge his thoughts of the offence, he may think and think so long, till he has *thought a distasteful apprehension into an action* of murder."—South, Serm. 9. p. 281. Vol. 10. ed. 1744. " For bring all the force of rhetoric in the world, yet *vice can never be praised into virtue.*"—Ibid. Serm. 8. p. 190. Vol. 8. This use of the preposition " into," with a like use, in a contrary sense, of the preposition " out of," occurs in South above a score times; so that a perusal of that Divine's sermons alone would train the reader to an easy recognition of Shakespeare's " telling a lie into truth." But although more frequent in South than any other writer, it is by no means peculiar to him. Ben Jonson in his " Time Vindicated" has:

" *Swears him into name,*
Upon his word and sword, for the sole youth
Dares make profession of poetic truth
Now militant amongst us."

And in his " Underwoods,"

> " Keep you such
> That I may love your person, as I do,
> Without your gift, though I can rate that too
> By *thanking thus the courtesy to life*
> Which you will bury."
>
> Epistle to Sir Edw. Sackville.

Of these illustrations of the syntax ascribed to " into" in the line quoted from the Tempest, the extract from the *Times* testifies to its continued use, and all of them corroborate it. " To tell a lie into truth," the language here attributed to Shakespeare is not a whit more forced or ungrammatical than " to discuss a frontier into familiarity," " to think an apprehension into an action," " to praise vice into virtue," " to swear a youth into name," or " to thank a courtesy to life."

Prospero's observation amounts to this; that a man may forge a lie, and repeat it until it passes with him into truth, his memory thereby losing at each repetition some part of its sense of the original falsehood, until it has, in that respect, become such a sinner, has so far transgressed its duty, and foregone its office, that the man credits the lie of which he had been himself the author. But surely we burn daylight; the lines are clearer than exposition; comment and paraphrase only obscure them. For those who reject the construction asserted here, and are still disposed to maintain that " sinner into truth" is right, it behoves them to furnish at least one sample of the usage they assume. They are to show that "a sinner into truth" is equivalent to "a sinner against truth." Let them then address themselves to the task, and to be successful, for it is not the work of a day, let them do so horse and foot, or in our grandsires' phrase, the meaning of which, as of very many other of their sayings, has perished with them, let them do so "for the heavens." In the meantime it will be safer with Halliwell, Dyce, and the Cambridge editors to repeal Heminge and Condell's banished text, which is much likelier to be genuine than the reading "unto" for "into," a corruption introduced by Warburton, and espoused by his successors of greatest note.

Vying with Warburton, Mr. Collier, in his attempt to expedite this knot, has by a further corruption knocked out the brains of the entire passage. What before imported but an error of construction he has sublimed into stark staring nonsense, not only not Shakespeare's sense, which theretofore had still been substantially saved, but into no man's sense, into sheer fatuity. It was universally admitted that according to Shakespeare a liar by lying made his memory a sinner against "truth;" no, prints Mr. Collier, in contempt of Shakespeare, of his editors, and commentators, and of all reason, "a sinner against untruth;" that is, a liar, by commission of it sins against the sin he commits; a sinner, by leasing trespasses against leasing, his sin; in a word, a sinner by the sin sins against the sin.

Referring to this improvement of Shakespeare by Collier, Mr. Staunton intimates that "it has not received the attention it deserves:" verily the Cambridge editors are absolved; Jackson and Beckett are not after all such scandals to criticism.

> "Those 'foolish' creatures yet do look well favoured
> When others are more 'foolish;' not being the worst
> Stands in some rank of praise."

Reckless of the absurdity entailed, and bent only upon obtaining an antecedent close at hand before the pronoun "it" Mr. Collier crops the syllable "un" from Warburton's "unto," and claps it before "truth." No doubt in this syllabic legerdemain there was a certain politic drift; for had not Steevens, Mason, Malone, and Knight pronounced the sentence to be ungrammatical or involved? Was not the pronoun "it" adjudged to be without a correlative? and does not the quintessence of Journal literature esteem Priscian's head more than a little scratched by relative and antecedent standing so far apart, and in preposterous order too? Sure Shakespeare was ill-advised to set "it," the pronoun, foremost, at the beginning, and "lie," its noun, hindmost, at the end of the sentence!

Now what may be forgiven to weakness offended by the unusual distance between noun and pronoun, and the postposition of the antecedent in Prospero's speech, becomes insufferable when a greater weak-

ness, in the absence of any stumbling-block, mounts
into the scorner's seat, and denounces as bad grammar this reversed order of noun and pronoun, or
relative and antecedent, although not only common
in every writer of our own language, good, bad, and
indifferent, but common in every language with
which we are acquainted.

In the *Saturday Review*, a periodical that numbers among its contributors, linguists, who, on their
own showing, might appear to have rocked the
cradle, and to understand the first lispings of articu-
late speech, to whom Psammitichus with his goats
is a mere novice in the origin of tongues, there may
be found every now and then supercilious glancings
at the grammar of its contemporaries. Thus in its
number of the 7th of Jan. '65, a cynic, snarling
at an article in the *Times* upon the disappearance
of the natives of Tasmania, fleers between brackets
at the grammatical composition of the following
sentence—"a charioteer who had been arrested by
the Emperor was very popular with them, (*the only
antecedent word is Thessalonica*) and the inhabitants
were therefore assembled at the Hippodrome under
the pretext of witnessing the races, and were then
barbarously massacred, &c."

To say nothing of the ignorance of the figure
metonymy betrayed by this critic, on finding in the
same article Attica represented by Athens, it is pitiable
to think that University training should disqualify a
pupil for seeing in "the inhabitants" an antecedent

D

to " them ;" that his classics, his *verbum personale*, should deprive him of all other notion of antecedency than what consists in a verbal sequence; that profundity and freedom of thought, the boastful prerogatives of your *Saturday Reviewer*, should be overawed and cowed by a term of art, and a grammatical symbol held paramount to the principles of which it, in common with others of the same mint, is but a lame and inadequate exponent. To be so logical it is a wonder that these writers stick so much in the rind of the letter of their grammar rules, that they are not on that very account led to a truer appreciation of the spirit of them. However it is quite obvious that the sagacity which is at fault, and cannot scent its way through the two particles " and the" to an antecedent for " them" of the *Times'* article, would have a hopeless hunt over a file of words eleven deep for an antecedent to " it" in the passage from the Tempest.

Conversant only with rectilinear stereotyped English, and for his theory of what it ought to be beholden to a style modelled upon his limited experience of what it is, your hide-bound scholar would make the " foot the tutor," just as though every custom in the common law of speech were over-ridden by certain compendious grammatical statutes, which are at most but declaratory of that, and being framed in general and comprehensive terms admit of a thousand exceptions: he does not understand that the marshalling of words, except in the most primitive and rudimentary essays, is not invariably regulated by their dependence on each other, as that is defined in syntactical formulæ : he is unfitted to apprehend how by the transposition of noun and pronoun, or relative and antecedent, inharmonious clumsiness of construction may be avoided, and thought kept on its way in more uninterrupted, evener flow, without sacrifice of lucidity. But he can libel Shakespeare, and his mother tongue ; he can prate, as if no one were capable of inditing current English without the intervention of their fescue whose childish puberty is not yet emancipated from the pedagogue's ferule.

If any think lightly of these verbal questions to which Shakespeare's text has given rise, or count the time spent on them ill bestowed, let him bethink him of the philosopher's maxim, τὰ ἐν τῇ φωνῇ τῶν ἐν τῇ ψυχῇ παθημάτων σύμβολα : let him reflect that words are both the canal and criteria of thought; that to ascertain a speaker's meaning you must first understand his speech; and that that will not be mastered, where either by gross anachronism the properties of a language at epochs three centuries apart are blindly confused, or its artless exorbitancies girthed with the strait belt of pedantic canons.

Successive expositors of Shakespeare have run tracing each other along the groove of both these errors, every fresh relay propagating the faults it inherited and bequeathing more of its own. Hence their commentaries are chiefly valuable, where they possess any value at all, for graduating the several stages of departure from its former self which the English language has travelled through since the days of Rowe, and for announcing the occasional recovery of superannuated idioms which at a later period has from time to time been achieved by some few of head-piece extraordinary. And yet it will not cost much pains to show that, with the command of libraries and of printing which we now enjoy, Shakespeare ought to be better edited, better understood, than he ever has been since his fellows Heminge and Condell first enriched their country with the dearest heirloom that it owns. This shall be the labour of the following chapters.